Design: Jill Coote
Recipe Photography: Peter Barry
Jacket and Illustration Artwork: Jane Winton,
courtesy of Bernard Thornton Artists, London
Editors: Jillian Stewart, Kate Cranshaw and Laura Potts

CLB 3513
Published by Grange Books,
an imprint of Grange Books PLC,
The Grange, Grange Yard, London.
© 1994 CLB Publishing,
Godalming, Surrey, England.
All rights reserved.
Printed and bound in Singapore
Published 1994
ISBN 1-85627-414-4

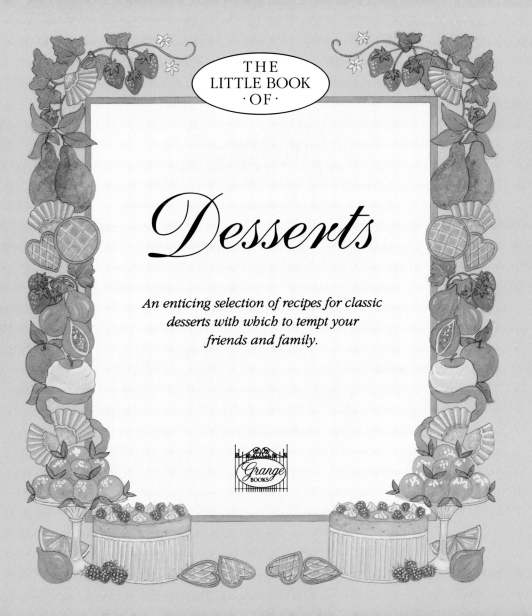

THE LITTLE BOOK ·OF·

Desserts

An enticing selection of recipes for classic desserts with which to tempt your friends and family.

Grange
BOOKS

Introduction

For many people a meal is not complete unless it is finished with something sweet, and they feel cheated if a dessert of some description is not on offer. Though the current trend is indisputably towards cutting down on sweet foods, with fresh fruit, cheese or low-calorie desserts replacing heavier puddings on a day-to-day basis, elaborate desserts still reign supreme on special occasions. A spectacular dessert gives the cook the opportunity to demonstrate their culinary skills and, as this will often be the part of the meal that people remember most vividly, seal their reputation as a good cook.

The word 'dessert', which comes from the French verb *desservir* meaning 'to clear the table', is defined in the dictionary as 'a usually sweet course served at the end of a meal'. Desserts as we know them did not become commonplace until the eighteenth century when refined sugar, the basis of so many sweet dishes, became more widely available in Europe. Until this time meals were usually completed with fresh and dried fruits, nuts and cheese. The first, simple desserts were either pies and tarts, which used pastry or dough to encase fruit, or custards and syllabubs made by combining eggs with sugar and milk or cream. Desserts became more sophisticated as the demands of high society in the eighteenth- and nineteenth-century became more rigorous and it was not uncommon for meals to end with a large variety of sweet dishes, including custards, pies, creams, cakes, pastries, meringues, gelatins, ice creams and hot puddings.

Modern kitchen equipment, particularly electric whisks and food processors, have taken much of the hard work out of preparing desserts and today's cook can produce some desserts in a fraction of the time that it would once have taken. More consistent oven temperatures and the ability to vary temperature at the touch of a button have also made it easier for the cook to produce the perfect result. This has meant that desserts that would once have been considered *haute cuisine* and would only have been attempted by an experienced chef can now be produced with relative ease at home.

This book features a selection of recipes for delicious desserts, including traditional British, Italian and French specialities, with which to delight your friends and family. Ranging from the simple and relatively low in calorie to the rich and utterly sinful, the recipes will provide inspiration for everything from a quick mid-week treat to that all-important finale to a celebration meal.

Parfait Au Cassis

SERVES 4

A rich and creamy dessert with a delicious fruity tang.

PREPARATION: 30 mins, plus freezing
COOKING: 30 mins

340g/12oz blackcurrants
2 tbsps crème de cassis
3 egg yolks
120g/4oz light muscovado sugar
280ml/½ pint single cream
280ml/½ pint double cream, whipped
Blackcurrants and mint leaves, to decorate

1. Purée the blackcurrants in a liquidizer or food processor and push through a sieve with a wooden spoon to remove the skin and pips. Add the cassis to the purée and freeze until it becomes slushy, stirring occasionally to prevent large ice crystals from forming.

2. Whisk the egg yolks and sugar together until they become very thick and mousse like.

Step 2 Whisk the egg yolks and sugar together until they become thick and mousse-like.

Step 3 Cool the mixture quickly by standing the bowl in iced water.

Heat the single cream in a small pan until almost but not quite boiling. Gradually add the cream to the egg mixture, stirring constantly.

3. Place the bowl over a pan of gently simmering water and cook, stirring constantly, until the mixture thickens. Cool quickly by standing the bowl in iced water, then fold in the whipped cream.

4. Freeze until the mixture is almost solid then beat with an electric mixer or in a food processor until slushy. Break up the blackcurrant mixture with a fork or electric whisk and fold into the cream mixture to give a marbled effect. Divide the mixture between 6 freezer-proof glasses and freeze until required.

5. Refrigerate for 30 minutes before serving, and decorate with blackcurrants and mint leaves.

Apple Nut Tart

SERVES 6

The sweet, spicy flavour of cinnamon blends perfectly with the apples and nuts in this traditional dessert.

PREPARATION: 20 mins
COOKING: 40 mins

250g/9oz plain flour
150g/5oz caster sugar
135g/4½oz butter, cut into pieces
1 egg
460g/1lb dessert apples, peeled, cored and
　　sliced
60g/2oz hazelnuts, coarsely ground
1 tsp ground cinnamon
Juice of 1 lemon
3 tbsps apricot brandy (optional)
120g/4oz apricot jam, melted
60g/2oz chopped hazelnuts

1. Sieve together the flour and 120g/4oz of the sugar into a bowl. Rub in the butter until the mixture resembles fine breadcrumbs.

Step 4 Layer the apples and ground hazelnuts in the pastry case.

Step 5 Pour the melted jam over the layers of apples and hazelnuts.

2. Make a well in the centre of the flour mixture and drop in the egg. Gradually incorporate the flour into the egg using a knife or, as the mixture becomes firmer, your fingers. Continue kneading the mixture together, until it forms a smooth dough.

3. Wrap the dough in cling film and chill for at least 30 minutes, then roll out and use it to line a 20cm/8-inch greased flan tin.

4. Layer the apple slices and the ground hazelnuts in the pastry case. Sprinkle over the cinnamon, remaining sugar, lemon juice and apricot brandy, if using.

5. Pour the melted jam over, and sprinkle with the chopped hazelnuts. Bake in a preheated oven at 220°C/425°F/Gas Mark 7, for 35-40 minutes or until the fruit is soft and the tart is golden brown.

Mocha Ice Cream Pie

MAKES 1 PIE

Unbelievably simple, yet incredibly delicious and impressive, this is a perfect ending to a summer meal.

PREPARATION: 25 mins, plus freezing

12 digestive biscuits
90g/3oz butter or margarine, melted
120g/4oz flaked coconut
60g/2oz plain chocolate, melted
850ml/1½ pints coffee ice cream

1. Crush biscuits with a rolling pin or in a food processor. Mix with melted butter or margarine.

2. Press into a 21.5cm/8½-inch spring-form tin. Chill thoroughly in the refrigerator.

3. Meanwhile, combine 30g/4 tbsps of the coconut with the melted chocolate. When cooled but not solidified, add about a quarter of the coffee ice cream, mixing well.

Step 2 Press the crust mixture into the base of a spring-form cake tin.

Step 5 Spread the coffee ice cream carefully over the chocolate-coconut layer and re-freeze.

4. Spread the mixture on top of the crust and freeze until firm.

5. Soften the remaining ice cream with an electric mixer or food processor and spread over the chocolate-coconut layer. Re-freeze until firm.

6. Toast the remaining coconut under a moderate grill, stirring frequently until pale golden brown. Allow to cool completely.

7. Remove the pie from the freezer and leave in the refrigerator for 30 minutes before serving. Push up the base of the tin and place the pie on a serving plate. Sprinkle the top with the toasted coconut. Cut into wedges to serve.

Zuppa Inglese

This is Italy's tribute to trifle. The name means English soup, but the custard is rich and thick.

PREPARATION: 25 mins plus chilling

2 tbsps cornflour
570ml/1 pint milk
2 eggs, lightly beaten
2 tbsps sugar
Grated rind of ½ lemon
Pinch nutmeg
460g/1lb ripe strawberries
16 sponge fingers
Amaretto liqueur
140ml/¼ pint double cream

1. Mix the cornflour with some of the milk. Beat the eggs, sugar, lemon rind and nutmeg together and pour in the remaining milk. Mix with the cornflour mixture in a heavy-based pan and stir over a gentle heat until the mixture thickens and comes to the boil.

Step 1
Combine the custard ingredients and cook until the mixture thickens and coats the back of a spoon.

Step 3 Place a layer of sponge fingers and strawberries in a serving dish and coat with a layer of custard. Repeat with remaining ingredients.

2. Allow to boil for 1 minute or until the mixture coats the back of a spoon. Place a sheet of greaseproof paper directly on top of the custard and allow it to cool slightly.

3. Save 8 even-sized strawberries for decoration and hull the remaining ones. Place half of the sponge fingers in the bottom of a glass bowl and sprinkle with some amaretto. Cut the strawberries in half and place a layer on top of the sponge fingers. Pour a layer of custard on top and repeat with the remaining sponge fingers and sliced strawberries. Top with another layer of custard and allow to cool completely.

4. Whip the cream and spread a thin layer over the top of the set custard. Pipe the remaining cream around the edge of the dish and decorate with the reserved strawberries. Serve chilled.

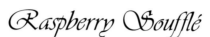

Raspberry Soufflé

SERVES 6

This light dessert is the perfect finale for a dinner party.

PREPARATION: 40 mins, plus chilling

460g/1lb raspberries
90g/3oz caster sugar
15g/½oz gelatine
140ml/¼ pint hot water
4 eggs, separated
280ml/½ pint double cream

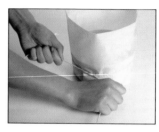

Step 1 Tie a sheet of greaseproof paper around the soufflé dish, to form a collar rising above the rim of the dish.

1. Prepare a 15cm/6-inch soufflé dish by tightly tying a lightly oiled sheet of greaseproof paper carefully around the outside edge of the soufflé dish, allowing it to stand approximately 10cm/4 inches above the rim of the dish.

2. Reserve a few of the raspberries for decoration, and purée the remainder with the sugar in a liquidiser or food processor.

3. Rub the puréed raspberries through a nylon sieve to remove the seeds.

4. Dissolve the gelatine in the hot water, stirring gently until it is completely dissolved and the liquid is clear.

5. Allow the gelatine to cool slightly and then beat it into the raspberry purée along with the egg yolks, mixing until all ingredients are well blended. Chill until partially set.

6. Whisk the egg whites until they form soft peaks.

7. Lightly whip half of the double cream until it is softly stiff.

8. Remove the partially set raspberry mixture from the refrigerator, and carefully fold in the cream and the egg whites using a metal tablespoon, blending lightly but thoroughly until the mixture is smooth.

9. Turn the mixture into the prepared dish – it should rise about 2.5cm/1-inch above the rim of the dish inside the paper collar. Allow to set in the refrigerator.

10. When completely set, carefully remove the collar and decorate the soufflé with the remaining whipped cream and the reserved raspberries.

Coffee Pecan Pie

SERVES 6-8

This traditional American pie is ideal for serving after a celebration meal.

PREPARATION: 20 mins, plus chilling

175g/6oz digestive biscuits, crushed
60g/2oz butter, melted
120g/4oz pecan nut halves
175g/6oz marshmallows
280ml/½ pint strong black coffee
15g/½oz gelatine
3 tbsps hot water
1 egg white
140ml/¼ pint fromage frais

---

1. Mix together the biscuit crumbs and the melted butter. Press onto the base and halfway up the sides of a well-greased 18cm/7-inch spring-form cake tin and chill for at least 1 hour.

2. Reserve 8 pecan nut halves for decoration, and chop the remainder finely.

3. In a large saucepan, dissolve the marshmallows in the coffee by heating gently

Step 2 Chop the remainder of the pecan nuts.

Step 3 Put the marshmallows and the coffee into a large saucepan, and heat gently, stirring until the marsh-mallows have dissolved.

and stirring frequently.

4. Sprinkle the gelatine onto the hot water and stir until it is clear and has dissolved.

5. Carefully pour the gelatine into the marsh-mallow mixture, and stir well, to ensure that it is evenly mixed in. Leave the marshmallow mixture to cool until it is almost set.

6. Whisk the egg white until it forms soft peaks, fold this into the fromage frais, and then fold this into the marshmallow mixture using a metal spoon to incorporate as much air as possible. Make sure all is evenly blended.

7. Stir in the chopped nuts and pour the mixture onto the chilled biscuit base. Chill the pie for at least 3 hours until completely set.

8. Remove the sides of the tin and slide the pie carefully onto a serving dish. Decorate with the reserved nut halves.

Chocolate Almond Stuffed Figs

SERVES 4

A positively luxurious pudding that is deceptively easy to prepare. Try it when an elegant sweet is called for.

PREPARATION: 20 mins
COOKING: 25 mins

---

4 ripe figs
2 tbsps liquid honey
30g/1oz unsweetened cooking chocolate
90g/3oz ground almonds

Cinnamon sauce
280ml/½ pint single cream
1 stick cinnamon
2 egg yolks
60g/4 tbsps sugar
Ground cinnamon and blanched almond
   halves, to garnish

Step 7
Combine cream and eggs and cook over gentle heat until mixture coats the back of a spoon.

1. Make a cross cut in each fig without cutting right down through the base. Carefully press the 4 sections of the fig out so that it looks like a flower.

2. Melt the honey and chocolate in a bowl over a pan of hot water.

3. Set aside to cool slightly and then mix in the ground almonds.

4. When the mixture has cooled completely, spoon an equal amount into the centre of each fig.

5. Meanwhile, prepare the sauce; pour the cream into a deep saucepan and add the cinnamon stick. Bring to just under the boil, draw off the heat and leave to infuse.

6. Beat the egg yolks and the sugar together until pale and thick, then gradually strain on the infused cream.

7. Return the mixture to the saucepan and stir over a gentle heat until it just coats the back of a spoon. Leave to cool until just warm.

8. To serve, pour a little of the custard onto each serving plate and tilt the plate slowly to coat the base. Place a filled fig on top of each and sprinkle around some of the ground cinnamon, topping each fig with a blanched almond.

Weinschaum

SERVES 4-6

This is a light and luscious pudding that can also be a sauce. Its name means "wine foam", which describes it perfectly.

PREPARATION: 15 mins, plus chilling

570ml/1 pint Rhine or Mosel wine
140ml/¼ pint water
4 eggs
120g/4oz sugar
Orange zest or crystallised rose or violet petals,
   for decoration

1. Place the wine and water in the top of a double boiler over boiling water. Make sure the top half of the double boiler does not actually

Step 2 Check the base of the bowl or double boiler. If very hot, place in a bowl of ice water and continue whisking.

Step 2 When thick enough, lift beaters or whisk and draw a trail of mixture across the bowl. It should stay and hold its shape on top.

touch the boiling water. Add the eggs and sugar and beat the ingredients vigorously with a wire whisk or an electric mixer.

2. When the custard thickens, it should hold a ribbon trail when the whisk or the beaters are lifted. Do not allow the custard to boil.

3. Spoon into serving dishes and decorate with strips of orange zest or crystallised flower petals. Serve hot or chill thoroughly before serving.

Frozen Lime and Blackcurrant Cream

SERVES 6

An impressive pudding that's perfect for entertaining.

PREPARATION: 40 mins, plus overnight freezing

Juice and zested rind of 4 limes
225g/8oz sugar
120g/4oz blackcurrants
3 egg whites
280ml/½ pint double cream, whipped

---

1. Measure the lime juice and make up to 90ml/3 fl oz with water if necessary.

2. Combine with the sugar in a heavy-based pan and bring to the boil slowly to dissolve the sugar.

3. When the mixture forms a clear syrup, boil rapidly to 120°C/248°F on a sugar thermometer.

4. Meanwhile, combine the blackcurrants with about 60ml/4 tbsps water in a small saucepan. Bring to the boil and then simmer, covered,

Step 5 Pour the syrup gradually onto the whisked egg whites, beating constantly.

Step 6 Fold the cream and the fruit purée into the egg whites, marbling the purée through the mixture.

until very soft. Purée, then sieve to remove the seeds and skin, and set aside to cool.

5. Whisk the egg whites until soft but not dry and then pour on the hot sugar syrup in a steady stream, whisking constantly. Add the lime rind and allow the meringue to cool.

6. When cold, fold in the whipped cream. Pour in the purée and marble through the mixture with a spatula. Do not over-fold. Pour the mixture into a lightly-oiled mould or bowl and freeze until firm.

7. Leave in the refrigerator for 30 minutes before serving or dip the mould in hot water for about 10 seconds. Place a plate over the bottom of the mould, invert and shake to turn out. Garnish with extra whipped cream and lime slices.

Tarte Tatin

SERVES 6-8

This classic French dessert is one of the tastiest ways of serving apples.

PREPARATION: 40 mins, plus chilling
COOKING: 20-25 mins

Pastry
200g/7oz plain flour
100g/3½oz butter, diced
1 egg yolk
2 tsps caster sugar
½ tsp salt
2 tsps water

90g/3oz butter
175g/6oz caster sugar
4 large apples, peeled, cored and quartered

1. To make the pastry, sift the flour onto a work surface. Make a well in the centre and add the remaining pastry ingredients to the well, mixing them together with your fingertips.

2. Gradually draw in the flour, until the mixture forms coarse crumbs, add a little extra water if necessary.

Step 5 Neatly pack the apples into the frying pan.

Step 6
Carefully lay the pastry over the apples, tucking the edges down inside the pan.

3. Draw the mixture into a ball then knead for 1-2 minutes on a lightly floured surface until smooth. Cover and chill for 30 minutes.

4. Melt the butter in a 25.5cm/10-inch flameproof and ovenproof frying pan, or tarte tatin tin.

5. Add the sugar and neatly pack in the apples. Cook for 15-20 minutes, until the sugar caramelizes. Then allow to cool slightly.

6. Roll the pastry out to a circle slightly larger than the pan. Place it over the apples, tucking the edges down inside the pan.

7. Bake in an oven preheated to 220°C/425°F/ Gas Mark 7, for 20-25 minutes or until the pastry is crisp and golden.

8. Allow to cool in the pan for 10 minutes, then turn out onto a serving plate and serve immediately with cream or crème fraîche.

Caramel Oranges

SERVES 4

This is one of the classic Italian sweets.

PREPARATION: 25 mins, plus chilling
COOKING: 25 mins

4 large oranges
275g/10oz sugar
400ml/14 fl oz water
2 tbsps brandy or orange liqueur

1. Use a swivel vegetable peeler to remove the rind from two of the oranges. Take off any white pith and cut the rind into very thin julienne strips with a sharp knife.

2. Place the julienne strips in a small saucepan, cover with water and bring to the boil. Drain then dry.

3. Cut the ends off all the oranges, then take the peel and pith off in very thin strips, using a sawing motion. Cut the oranges horizontally into slices about 5mm/¼-inch thick.

Step 1 Peel the oranges in thin strips with a vegetable peeler. Remove any white pith and cut into thin julienne strips.

Step 3 Use a serrated knife to take off orange peel in thin strips.

4. Stir the sugar and 340ml/12 fl oz of the water in a heavy-based pan over medium heat until the sugar has dissolved. Add the drained orange peel strips to the pan.

5. Boil the syrup gently, uncovered, for about 10 minutes or until the orange strips are glazed. Remove the strips from the pan and place on a lightly oiled plate.

6. Return the pan to a high heat and boil, uncovered, until it turns a pale golden brown. Remove from the heat immediately and quickly add the remaining water. Return to a gentle heat for a few minutes to dissolve the hardened caramel, then allow to cool completely. Stir in the brandy.

7. Arrange the orange slices in a serving dish and pour over the cooled syrup. Pile the glazed orange strips on top and refrigerate for several hours, or overnight, before serving.

Fresh Fruit in Tulip Cups

SERVES 4

Elegant presentation is what gives this simple fruit dessert its special, dinner-party touch.

PREPARATION: 10 mins, plus 1 hr standing
COOKING: 8-10 mins

Tulip cups
1 egg white
60g/2oz sugar
30g/1oz plain flour
30g/1oz butter, melted
30g/1oz ground almonds
1 tbsp flaked almonds

Fruit filling
1 mango
2 figs
10 strawberries
1 kiwi
10 cherries
Vanilla ice cream
1 tbsp flaked almonds

1. To make the tulip cups, mix the egg white with the sugar, then add the flour, melted butter and the ground almonds, beating well to incorporate all the ingredients. Set aside to rest for 1 hour.

2. Peel the fruit as necessary and cut into attractive shapes.

3. Place 1 tbsp of the batter on a non-stick

Step 5 When the biscuits are still hot, mould them by pressing them into small bowls so they have crinkled edges.

baking sheet, and spread it out well using the back of a spoon. Repeat three times. Sprinkle over the flaked·almonds, dividing them equally between the four rounds.

4. Cook in an oven preheated to 200°C/400°F/Gas Mark 6, for 8-10 minutes, until lightly brown.

5. When cooked, and while they are still hot, mould the biscuits by pressing them into brioche tins or small bowls. Allow them to cool and harden in the moulds.

6. When cool, remove the tulip cups from their moulds and place on serving plates. Fill with the fruit, top with a little vanilla ice cream and decorate with the remaining 1 tbsp flaked almonds.

Apricot Fool

SERVES 4

This dish makes a very quick and easy dessert.

PREPARATION: 10 mins, plus soaking
COOKING: 30 mins

225g/8oz dried apricots
1 ripe banana
200g/7oz carton Greek yogurt
1 egg, separated
Chocolate curls

1. Soak the apricots in water for at least 1 hour. Simmer in the water for 20-30 minutes or until tender, then remove with a slotted spoon to a blender or food processor and purée until smooth.

2. Mash the banana and add to the apricot purée.

3. Fold the yogurt into the fruit mixture along with the egg yolk.

4. Whisk the egg white until stiff then gently fold into the fruit mixture. Spoon into individual glasses and chill. Decorate with curls of chocolate or toasted almonds.

Poires au Vin Rouge

SERVES 6

A marvellous recipe for using firm cooking pears to their best advantage.
They look beautiful served in a glass bowl.

PREPARATION: 25 mins
COOKING: 20 mins

570ml/1 pint dry red wine
Juice of ½ lemon
1 strip lemon peel
225g/8oz sugar
1 small piece stick cinnamon
6 small ripe but firm pears, peeled, but with the
  stalks left on

---

1. Bring the wine, lemon juice and peel, sugar and cinnamon to the boil in a deep saucepan or flameproof casserole in which the pears fit snugly. Stir until the sugar dissolves and then allow to boil rapidly for 1 minute.

2. Peel the pears lengthwise and remove the small eye from the bottom of each pear. Place

Step 2 Peel the pears lengthwise and remove the eye from the bottom.

Step 2 Place the pears in the simmering wine, upright or on their sides.

the pears upright in the simmering wine. Allow to cook slowly for 20 minutes, or until they are soft but not mushy. If the syrup does not completley cover the pears, allow the pears to cook on their sides and turn and baste them frequently. Cool the pears in the syrup until lukewarm and then remove them. Remove the cinnamon stick and the lemon peel and discard.

3. If the syrup is still very thin, remove pears, boil to reduce slightly or mix 1 tbsp arrowroot with a little cold water, add some of the warm syrup and return the arrowroot to the rest of the syrup. Bring to the boil, stirring constantly until thickened and cleared. Spoon the syrup over the pears and refrigerate or serve warm. Decorate with flaked toasted almonds and serve with lightly whipped cream if wished.

Vanilla Cream Melba

SERVES 4

Pasta is wonderful in desserts as it soaks up flavours beautifully.

PREPARATION: 15 mins, plus chilling
COOKING: 10 mins

90g/3oz soup pasta
420ml/¾ pint milk
45g/1½oz brown sugar
Few drops vanilla essence
140ml/¼ pint cream, lightly whipped
1 large can peach halves
1 tsp cinnamon (optional)

Melba sauce
225g/8oz raspberries
30g/1oz icing sugar

Step 2 Fold cream into cooled pasta mixture.

Step 4 Serve pasta with peach halves.

1. Cook the pasta in the milk and sugar until tender. Stir regularly, being careful not to allow it to boil over.

2. Draw off the heat and stir in vanilla essence. Pour the pasta into a bowl and allow to cool. When cool, fold in the cream and leave to chill in the refrigerator.

3. Meanwhile, make the Melba sauce. Purée the raspberries in a blender or food processor, then push the purée through a fine nylon sieve. Mix in some icing sugar to taste.

4. Serve the pasta in shallow dishes. Set the peach halves on top and drizzle over the Melba sauce. Dust with cinnamon if wished.

Lemon and Ginger Cheesecake

SERVES 6-8

This fresh, creamy-tasting cheesecake is full of wholesome ingredients.

PREPARATION: 30 mins, plus chilling

45g/1½oz butter, melted
30g/1oz soft brown sugar
90g/3oz wholemeal biscuits, crushed
175g/6oz curd cheese
2 eggs, separated
Finely grated rind 1 lemon
30g/1oz soft brown sugar
140ml/¼ pint natural yogurt
15g/½oz powdered gelatine
3 tbsps hot water
Juice ½ lemon
3 pieces preserved stem ginger, rinsed in warm
    water and chopped
60ml/4 tbsps thick natural yogurt

1. Mix the melted butter with the sugar and crushed biscuits. Press the mixture evenly over the base of a greased 18cm/7-inch loose-

Step 1 Spread the biscuit crumb mixture evenly over the base of the flan dish, drawing it slightly up the sides of the dish.

Step 4 Thoroughly mix in the dissolved gelatine, along with the lemon juice.

bottomed flan tin and chill for at least an hour.

2. Beat the curd cheese with the egg yolks, lemon rind and sugar. Stir in the yogurt.

3. Dissolve the gelatine in the water, and add this to the cheese mixture, stirring thoroughly, to incorporate evenly.

4. Stir in the lemon juice, and put the cheese mixture to one side until it is on the point of setting.

5. Whisk the egg whites until they are stiff but not dry, and fold them lightly, but thoroughly, into the cheese mixture together with the chopped ginger. Spoon into the prepared flan dish, smoothing the surface.

6. Chill the cheesecake for 3-4 hours, until the filling has set completely. Swirl the natural yogurt over the top and decorate with julienne strips of lemon zest, or lemon twists.

Summer Pudding

SERVES 6

*This dessert must be prepared at least 24 hours before it is needed and is an
excellent way of using up a glut of soft summer fruits.*

PREPARATION: 30 mins, plus overnight chilling

900g/2lb mixed soft fruit (raspberries,
redcurrants, blackcurrants, cherries,
strawberries)
8-10 thick slices day-old white bread, with
crusts removed
120g/4oz caster sugar (more or less can be used
according to taste)

1. Prepare and wash fruit and place in a heavy-
based saucepan together with the caster sugar.
Cook over a low heat until the sugar dissolves
and the juices start to run.

2. Line the base and sides of a greased 850ml/
1½ pint pudding basin with some of the slices
of bread, trimmed to fit the shape of the bowl
tightly. Pack in the fruit and a little of the juice
to stain the bread.

3. Cover with the remaining slices, pour on a
little more juice and retain the rest. Cover the
basin with a saucer or plate which rests on the
pudding itself.

4. Add a 460g/1lb weight or heavy tin or jar, in
order to compress the pudding. Leave to stand
overnight in the refrigerator or a cool place.

5. To turn out, loosen the sides with a palette
knife and invert onto a serving plate. Use the
remaining juice to stain any white patches of
bread and serve with double or clotted cream.

Brown Bread Ice Cream

SERVES 4

This unusual ice cream is easy to make and is an ideal standby dessert to keep in the freezer.

PREPARATION: 40 mins, plus freezing

---

2 egg yolks
60g/2oz caster sugar
420ml/¾ pint double, or whipping cream
Few drops of vanilla essence
225ml/8 fl oz water
175g/6oz soft brown sugar
25g/6 tbsps fresh brown breadcrumbs
1 tsp ground cinnamon

---

1. Put the egg yolks and the caster sugar into a bowl, and whisk vigorously with an electric beater until thick, pale and creamy.

2. Pour in the double cream and continue whisking until thick and creamy.

3. Beat in the vanilla essence, then pour the cream mixture into a shallow freezer-proof container and freeze for 1 hour, or until beginning to set around the edges.

4. Break the ice cream away from the edges and whisk with the electric beater until the ice crystals have broken up. Return to the freezer for a further hour. Repeat this procedure 2 more times, then freeze completely.

5. Put the water and brown sugar into a small saucepan and heat gently, stirring until the sugar has dissolved. Bring the mixture to the

Step 6 When cooled, the caramelised breadcrumbs should set completely hard.

boil and boil rapidly until the sugar caramelises.

6. Remove the caramel sugar from the heat and stir in the breadcrumbs and the cinnamon. Spead the mixture onto a baking sheet lined with oiled greaseproof paper, and allow to set.

7. Break up the caramelised breadcrumbs by placing them in a plastic food bag and crushing with a rolling pin.

8. Turn the frozen ice cream into a large bowl and break it up with a fork. Allow to soften slightly, then stir in the caramelised breadcrumbs, mixing thoroughly to blend evenly.

9. Return the ice cream to the freezer tray and freeze completely. Allow the mixture to soften for 10 minutes before serving in scoops with crisp biscuits.

Index

Apple Nut Tart 10
Apricot Fool 32
Brown Bread Ice Cream 42
Caramel Oranges 28
Chocolate Almond Stuffed Figs 20
Coffee Pecan Pie 18
Fresh Fruit in Tulip Cups 30
Frozen Lime and Blackcurrant Cream 24
Fruit:
    Caramel Oranges 28
    Chocolate Almond Stuffed Figs 20
    Fresh Fruit in Tulip Cups 30
    Poires au Vin Rouge 34
    Summer Pudding 40
Ice Cream:
    Brown Bread Ice Cream 42
    Frozen Lime and Blackcurrant
        Cream 24
    Mocha Ice Cream Pie 12
Lemon and Ginger Cheesecake 38
Mocha Ice Cream Pie 12

Mousses and Fools:
    Apricot Fool 32
    Parfit au Cassis 8
    Raspberry Soufflé 16
    Weinschaum 22
Parfit au Cassis 8
Poires au Vin Rouge 34
Puddings:
    Vanilla Cream Melba 36
    Zuppa Inglese 14
Raspberry Soufflé 16
Summer Pudding 40
Tarte Tatin 26
Tarts and Pies:
    Apple Nut Tart 10
    Coffee Pecan Pie 18
    Lemon and Ginger Cheesecake 38
    Tarte Tatin 26
Vanilla Cream Melba 36
Weinschaum 22
Zuppa Inglese 14